The
Down-to-Earth Guide to
Global Warming

The
Down-to-Earth Guide to
Global Warming

Laurie David and Cambria Gordon

ORCHARD BOOKS • NEW YORK
AN IMPRINT OF SCHOLASTIC INC.

All rights reserved. Published by Orchard Books, an imprint of Scholastic Inc.,
Publishers since 1920. ORCHARD BOOKS and design are registered trademarks of
Watts Publishing Group, Ltd., used under license. SCHOLASTIC and associated logos
are trademarks and/or registered trademarks of Scholastic Inc.

The publisher has made diligent efforts to trace ownership of all copyrighted material
in this volume and believes that all necessary permissions have been secured. If
there are any questions regarding the use of these materials, the publisher will take
appropriate corrective measures to acknowledge ownership in future editions.

Library of Congress Cataloging-in-Publication Data

David, Laurie. Gordon, Cambria.

The Down-to-Earth Guide to Global Warming / by Laurie David and Cambria Gordon.

p. cm.

ISBN-13: 978-0-439-02494-5
ISBN-10: 0-439-02494-3

1. Global warming—Juvenile literature. I. Gordon, Cambria. II. Title.

QC981.8.G56D38 2007

363.738'74—dc22

2006035705

10 9 8 7 6 5 4 3 2 1   07 08 09 10 11
Printed in the U.S.A.   03

First edition, September 2007

Book Design by Charles Kreloff

Text is printed on FSC-certified paper
that is 100% post-consumer waste.

Recycled
Supporting responsible use
of forest resources
www.fsc.org Cert no. SW-COC-2082
© 1996 Forest Stewardship Council

For Cazzie and Romy, so that they can finally
understand what I have been talking about, and
to the staff at the Natural Resources Defense
Council — more than 300 lawyers, scientists, and
policy experts who have devoted their lives to
protecting our environment

— L. D.

For Micah, Arlo, and Capp, who keep me down to
Earth, and for Laurie, who opened my eyes

— C. G.

Acknowledgments

They say that it takes a village to raise a child. Well, the authors believe that it also takes a village to write a children's book. We could not have completed this book without the help of so many. First and foremost, a thank-you to our husbands, Larry and Howard, who have supported our passion for the environment with both humor and love. Thank you to the experts at the Natural Resources Defense Council: Allen Hershkowitz, Andrew Wetzler, Darby Hoover, Jack Murphy, Jon Coifman, Kate Wing, Lisa Suatoni, Luke Tonachel, Nathanial Greene, and especially the ever-patient Dan Lashof, Joel Reynolds, John Steelman, and Tim Greeff for the extra time they put in to help us understand the complexities of global warming; Susan Hassol for her endless reads and thoughtful scientific assessments; Brendan DeMelle and Rachel Diamond, the best researchers any authors could ask for; Dawn Woollen and Sara Altshul for their superb attention to detail; Liana Schwarz for her unlimited knowledge, patience, and coordination of our fact-checking; Eric Wolff, Dr. Gareth Marshall, and the scientists at British Antarctic Survey; Heidi Cullen of the Weather Channel, for her grasp of wacky weather; Richard Fox of the Butterfly Conservation; Erica Levine of Community Energy, Inc.; David Zutler of Biota, for kindly responding to our inquiries; Cristina Mittermeier, Executive Director, International League of Conservation Photographers, for her willingness to lend images to this book ; and Dr. Mark Spencer, Director of the Environmental Leadership Opportunity Program College of Natural Resources UC Berkeley. Grateful acknowledgment is made to Reggie Bush, Cedric the Entertainer, Sheryl Crow, Leonardo DiCaprio, Jennifer Garner, Laird Hamilton, Jim Lovell, and Shaun White for their participation and insightful comments. Much appreciation goes to Judy Rothman for the impetus to do a cool kids' project on the environment; to Jennifer Jaeger at Andrea Brown Literary Agency for her undying belief in this book; Brian Lipson at Endeavor for his astute pro bono legal counsel; our gracious editor, Lisa Sandell, for her insightful comments, flag-waving enthusiasm, and vision; Amla Sanghvi, photo editor extraordinaire; Siobhán McGowan, for helping bring this book to fruition; and the incredible members of the Scholastic design team, Charles Kreloff, Kay Petronio, David Saylor, and Becky Terhune, who brought our vision to life.

Contents

1
It's Getting Hot in Here

2
Weird, Wacky Weather

3
Extinction Stinks

4
What You Can Do to Stop Global Warming

Boldface indicates a term defined in the Words to Know section on page 100.

Authors' Note

Since this book was written, much has happened and breaking news stories about global warming are coming fast. Here are some big developments that we learned about right as we were going to press:

The United States Supreme Court ruled that carbon dioxide and other global warming emissions are indeed pollutants under the Clean Air Act, so the Environmental Protection Agency has the authority to start cutting them. This is good news for the planet!

The Intergovernmental Panel on Climate Change (IPCC), a group made up of hundreds of scientists from around the world, concluded in its latest report that the warming of the climate system is unequivocal and very likely due to human activity. The third installment of IPCC's four-part report echoes the Stern Report, issued in England, which concluded that the costs of stabilizing the planet are significant but manageable and that the longer we wait, the more costly and dangerous it will become.

Scientists at the National Ice and Snow Center of Colorado, using satellite data and visual confirmation, found the polar ice cap to be melting much faster — 30 years faster! — than the IPCC predicted.

China is expected to surpass the United States as the number one source of global warming emissions in the next year or two.

A diverse group of corporations from around the world, including General Electric, Air France, Volvo, and Citigroup, have formed the Global Round Table on Climate Change. This nonpolitical coalition is asking its governments to set targets to reduce CO_2 emissions. Similarly, corporations in the United States, including General Motors, PepsiCo, Royal Dutch Shell's U.S. subsidiary, BP America, ConocoPhillips, and Johnson & Johnson, have formed the United States Climate Action Partnership. They are also asking Congress to limit greenhouse gas emissions. This is especially notable because many of these corporations are in the oil and gas business!

Australia and Canada have voted to ban the use of regular incandescent lightbulbs by 2009 and 2012, respectively.

The city of San Francisco voted to outlaw the use of plastic checkout bags in large supermarkets by Fall 2007 and in large chain pharmacies about six months after that. In the United States and Canada, some of the biggest retailers, including Home Depot, Wal-Mart, and Ikea, are taking steps to promote sustainable products and reduce the carbon footprint of their stores.

As our Earth continues to show signs of global warming, people are showing signs of action. We salute you.

Dear Reader,

We are proud to present *The Down-to-Earth Guide to Global Warming*. This book was born out of our desire for kids to know the truth about this problem and what they can do to help solve it. The consequences of global warming are seen every day in extreme weather events, in the news media, and in our own backyards. It can be scary not understanding global warming, especially if we don't know how to be part of the effort to solve it. On a personal note, as moms, we have the responsibility to make sure that in the years to come, when we are asked by our own children, *what did you know, when did you know it, and what did you do?*, we are able to answer these questions.

    The Down-to-Earth Guide to Global Warming is divided into four parts. The first deals with the science of global warming and explains why it happens and how we arrived at our present situation. The second talks about the effect global warming is having on our weather systems. The third part focuses on global warming's impact on plant and animal life, while the final section covers, among other things, the many steps kids, along with their parents, teachers, and friends, can take to help reverse this problem.

    There has never been a more important time to talk about global warming and to take action. Every person on this planet, young or old, has a part to play. By reading this book and giving it to others to read, you're becoming a part of the solution, too.

We hope this book will inspire you to help stop global warming!

Sincerely,

Laurie David   *Cambria Gordon*

Laurie David and Cambria Gordon
Los Angeles, California, 2007

The
Down-to-Earth Guide to
Global Warming

Part 1
It's Getting Hot in Here

So What Exactly *Is* Global Warming?

Picture this: It's late at night. You're asleep in bed, with lots of blankets covering you. Suddenly, you wake up all hot and sweaty, so you kick off the covers. Cool air hits your legs. Much better. You fall back to sleep and wake up refreshed, ready for school.

Now picture the Earth. Certain gases that have been collecting in the atmosphere for the past 100 years are creating a heavy blanket around the Earth. **Heat from the sun gets trapped under the blanket and the Earth begins to feel too hot. But the Earth can't just kick off that cover to cool down. This is global warming.**

Of all the gases in the atmosphere, carbon dioxide (CO_2) contributes the most to global warming. But CO_2 is also necessary to sustain life. CO_2 is released into the atmosphere when dead organisms decompose and volcanoes erupt. It is then absorbed by plants, which use it to grow, and by the oceans, which use it to nourish sea life, beginning with microscopic plants called algae.

Our planet is heating up.

2

Humans and other animals eat plants and exhale carbon dioxide when they breathe, completing the cycle. And over thousands and millions of years, much of this carbon ends up buried underground or at the bottom of the oceans.

Every living thing on planet Earth is part of the natural carbon cycle.

This is how it has always worked. But, recently, we have been asking too much of the carbon cycle. **Cars, factories, and electric power plants have been putting too much of this buried carbon into our atmosphere.**

You might be thinking, why is global warming so important now? Well, because the Earth is the only home we have. When weather patterns are altered, life as we know it will be altered, too. We'll feel the changes every season of the year, while at home or on vacation. For example, global warming is causing some summer nights to be as warm as summer days, preventing people's bodies from getting a necessary break from the heat, and this creates serious health risks. Global warming is also causing less snow to fall in the higher altitudes, so your favorite ski and snowboard spot might be closed when you get there.

Global warming is a problem that's happening now. The good news is that we still have time to solve it.

While the Earth is indeed good at absorbing carbon dioxide, it can only handle so much. If carbon dioxide were a pizza, then we are expecting the Earth to eat a whole pie rather than just one slice. In other words, we're releasing too much carbon dioxide, too fast.

A Greenhouse Gas Is Not Caused by an Orchid Grower Who Ate Too Many Beans

That would be gas in the greenhouse.

I f you've ever eaten too many burritos, then you know what can happen afterward. But we're not talking about that kind of gas. The gases we're talking about have been floating around in our atmosphere, surrounding the Earth, since life first began. **Greenhouse gases have names like carbon dioxide, methane (which, now that you mention it, burping and farting cows actually help produce), water vapor, nitrous oxide, and more.**
The reason they're called greenhouse gases is because they act just like a real glass-covered greenhouse, like the kind you could grow orchids in — or even beans. Both glass-covered greenhouses and greenhouse gases let sunlight in but prevent the warmth from escaping back out.

What Kinds of Greenhouse Gases Are Polluting Our Air?

Carbon Dioxide 82%

Methane 9%

Nitrous Oxide 5%

Other 4%

Ever wonder where some of that methane comes from?

A little bit of greenhouse gas is good. It keeps our planet at a comfortable 57°F (14°C), a temperature that's averaged over the whole planet and across all the seasons. But at this point in history, we humans have released so much greenhouse gas into the atmosphere, the Earth's average temperature has actually risen one degree! Maybe you're thinking that doesn't sound so bad.

If the Earth's average temperature increases even a few degrees, gigantic changes can happen:

🌼 Glaciers will melt.

🌼 Oceans will get too warm, causing fiercer hurricanes.

🌼 Animals and plants might die because they can't adapt to the change in temperature.

🌼 And humans can suffer, too.

Too bad the Earth can't just stop eating burritos.

Consider this:

You know that Popsicle in your freezer? At 32°F (0°C), it freezes and stays solid enough for you to bite it. But at 33°F (0.5°C), it falls off the stick.

The Greenhouse Effect

Normal Greenhouse Effect

When direct sunlight (**short-wave energy**) heads toward Earth, it passes right through greenhouse gases. Some of the sunlight is reflected by the clouds back into space, but most is absorbed by the Earth and is used to warm the planet's surface. The Earth then radiates some of that heat (**long-wave energy**) back into the atmosphere. Only then do greenhouse gases go to work, trapping long-wave energy and using it to keep the lower ten miles of our atmosphere livable.

Extreme Greenhouse Effect

With the increased amount of greenhouse gases in our atmosphere, too much long-wave energy is being trapped underneath the greenhouse blanket. The extra heat has nowhere to go but back down to Earth, warming the planet more than is healthy.

5

Were Fossil Fuels Once Dinosaurs?

If you've ever gone fossil hunting, then you know the thrill of finding a sea-snail shell or a rock with a leaf print embedded in it from millions of years ago. Well, what if you went fossil hunting and found a piece of coal? Or a drop of black oil? Even though it's highly unlikely, it's possible, because coal, oil, and natural gas were buried deep in the ground around the time of the dinosaurs. That's why they're called **fossil fuels**. But before we get ahead of ourselves, let's start at the beginning.

More than 300 million years ago, even before dinosaurs roamed the Earth, the land was covered with large trees, leafy plants, swamps, and oceans. In the water lived algae — tiny sea creatures ranging in size from a single cell to many cells. As our bodies need fat and carbohydrates for energy and growth, so do algae. We get our energy from the food we eat; algae get it from the sun. Algae use sunlight to convert carbon dioxide into carbohydrates, storing energy for growth. But they also store something else. Oil. **A microscopic amount of oil is present in all algae!**

When the prehistoric algae died, as all living things eventually do, they sank to the bottom of the water. They were then buried, either by sea or by **sediment**, which is a mishmash of sand, clay, and other minerals. Maybe an earthquake shook the ground so hard that sediment eventually covered an entire swamp, or an ice age came along suddenly and froze an ocean for thousands of years. However it happened, the algae lay there, buried.

Now, three miles (5 km) of seawater or dirt over your microscopic head can get pretty heavy. It can get hot, too.

The deeper you go toward the center of the Earth, as you approach what's called the mantle, the hotter it gets.

Also, heat is always released when dead matter decomposes. Well, it got very hot around all those dead algae, like an oven of sorts. And through time, this heat, along with the weight of the water and sediment, put pressure on the dead algae and squeezed it like your brother might squeeze your arm. This squeezing forced out the stored fat and carbohydrates from the algae, as well as the oil that was already there, and trapped it underground, where it turned into the black stuff — petroleum — that we use today to power our cars.

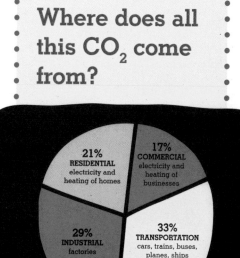

Where does all this CO_2 come from?

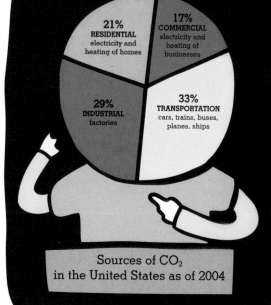

21%
RESIDENTIAL
electricity and heating of homes

17%
COMMERCIAL
electricity and heating of businesses

29%
INDUSTRIAL
factories

33%
TRANSPORTATION
cars, trains, buses, planes, ships

Sources of CO_2 in the United States as of 2004

Coal and natural gas, our two other fossil fuels, have slightly different origins. Coal started out as fallen forest trees and plant material that, over time, were also buried. Just like the energy that was forced out of the algae, heat and pressure forced water out from the dead plant material, leaving only a carbohydrate-filled mixture that looked a lot like dark paste, called peat. Over millions of years, the peat hardened into coal. Today, coal is mainly used to provide electricity.

Natural gas, or methane, originates from dead swamp matter that decomposed deeper down in the Earth than its oil counterpart. So deep, in fact, that no oxygen was present. (Oil is usually found closer to the Earth's surface than natural gas.) Chemicals like carbon and hydrogen were also squeezed out of the dead swamp matter, and the high heat and lack of oxygen caused a chemical reaction, changing the energy stored in the dead organic matter into natural gas. Today, natural gas is used to heat our homes and light our stoves.

It took millions of years for the three types of fossil fuels — oil, coal, and natural gas — to form, but humans have taken them out of the ground in a fraction of the time! And this is precisely where global warming fits in. All those prehistoric algae, plants, and dead matter were storing energy in the form of carbon. And what happens when you burn a fossil fuel? Its carbon combines with oxygen to become carbon dioxide, which is then released into the atmosphere.

The burning of fossil fuels is the biggest contributor to greenhouse gases and, therefore, the biggest contributor to global warming. And we do a lot of burning on this planet.

So the answer to the question at the start of this chapter is yes, today's oil, coal, and natural gas were once prehistoric algae, plants, and maybe some skin cells from a *Tyrannosaurus rex*. But the thing that makes fossil fuels truly like dinosaurs is that, with all the new, cleaner technologies people are beginning to discover and use, our dependence on dirty fossil fuels should become a thing of the past — and stay there.

A miner in Colorado extracts coal that will be burned later at a power plant.

You Say You Want a Revolution?

R evolution is an enormous change that occurs in history. People may fight against their leaders to change their governments. Or, on a smaller scale, if you wanted to have french fries in the cafeteria instead of broccoli, then you could try revolting. (A peaceful protest works wonders.) A revolution doesn't always have to occur by force. It can also happen because people make great changes in the way they do things. This happened in Great Britain in the 1750s, when the Industrial Revolution began.

Before the middle of the 1700s, people made most things by hand. Take that shirt you're wearing, for example. If you lived in the countryside of England in 1740, you probably used your fingers to comb the wool fibers that were sheared off a sheep. Once the fibers were all parallel and untangled, you then spun or twisted them, and threaded them onto a loom to make the cloth. This whole process took almost a week! But, in 1786, a man named Edmund Cartwright figured out a way to make a power loom that could do all that work in a matter of hours! **Once people tasted the sweet life of speed and efficiency, they didn't want to go back to doing things by hand again.**

By the mid-1800s, the Industrial Revolution had spread to North America, Japan, and beyond. It was an exciting

It's time for a new *clean,* *green* industrial revolution.

10

time, filled with a sense that anything was possible. Innovation and creativity popped up in unexpected places. A poor man could become a millionaire: All it took was one great idea. Steam engines powered the trains that crisscrossed the United States and revolutionized travel and shipping. Automobiles came next, with their internal combustion engines. Then Thomas Edison invented the first incandescent lightbulb, bringing electricity into the home. Electric power plants sprang up all over, burning coal to boil water into steam that would power the generators. Industry made people's lives easier. Millions of jobs were created and people prospered.

Nobody knew back then that all this industrial progress would end up changing the natural patterns of our climate. In fact, many scientists believe the Industrial Revolution was actually the start of global warming, because that's when we began burning fossil fuels in large quantities. *Now* **we know.**

Knowing doesn't mean you have to give up that shirt on your back or your ride to the mall or your reading light. Knowing doesn't mean the end of modern conveniences. And it certainly doesn't mean the end of jobs and prosperity. In fact, it's just the opposite. Knowing means a change in thinking that lets us power our lives differently.

What Is Green?

Besides the color you turn after riding a roller coaster ten times in a row, **green** traditionally represents nature and the richness of life on our planet. This is certainly one reason why the word has been adopted to describe everything that seeks to protect and preserve the well-being of people and the planet — from politics to products in your grocery store.

CO$_2$: The Big Kahuna

The year was 1958. In Hawaii, while most people were catching waves, a young scientist named Charles David Keeling climbed to the top of Mauna Loa, a mountain volcano high above the surf. There he planted a manometer, a device he invented to measure the gnarliest greenhouse gas of all: carbon dioxide. For one year, Keeling took a daily measurement of CO$_2$ concentration in the atmosphere. When he graphed his measurements, Keeling found that in the summer, carbon dioxide levels dipped down low because there were so many trees and plants that bloomed in the spring. All those extra leaves did just what they were supposed to: take CO$_2$ from the atmosphere and combine it with sunlight and a green pigment called chlorophyll to give themselves energy (aka photosynthesis).

The Keeling Curve

The Keeling Curve illustrates the concentration of CO_2 in the atmosphere, measured atop Mauna Loa, Hawaii, 1958–2005.

CO_2 Concentration in Parts Per Million (PPM)

Year

In the winter months, when the plants and trees shed their leaves, CO_2 levels increased because there was not as much photosynthesis going on, which means a lot less CO_2 was being consumed. Nature was doing its job.

The seasons were turning and the trees and plants were reacting perfectly. Keeling was so fascinated by these seasonal reflections of CO_2 concentrations that he continued taking measurements for three decades. It wasn't long before Keeling noticed something radical. The angle of the graph kept going up. The wintertime highs of CO_2 concentrations were getting higher and the summertime lows were not dipping down as low.

The amount of CO_2 in the Earth's atmosphere was rising every year.

What a discovery! The Keeling Curve became a famous image and is now accepted by scientists and surfers all over the world. Kowabunga.

How in the World Does Photosynthesis Work?

Photosynthesis is the way in which plants create food for themselves. Using a green pigment called chlorophyll, plants take energy from the sun and combine it with CO_2 and water to make sugar, which in turn gives them sustenance. The plants then release oxygen as a by-product. In other words, plants are keeping the carbon, but releasing the dioxide!

Fact: One tree can absorb the amount of CO_2 released by an average car that's been driven for 4,000 miles (6,437 km).

The Mystery of the Dome C Ice Core

The scientists from the British Antarctic Survey (BAS) are real-life sleuths who have uncovered clues to what weather was like hundreds of thousands of years ago. Wearing bear-paws (gloves) and mukluks (boots), they battle temperatures 40°F below zero (-40°C) in the harshest climate on Earth. In 2004, the folks from BAS drilled into the East Antarctica ice, at a spot called Dome C. Using a drill just four inches (10 cm) wide, they ground their way downward, separating a skinny column of ice and drawing it toward the surface. When they were done, they had gone more than two miles (3 km) down into the ice. That column of ice, called an ice core, dated back 650,000 years in time!

After studying the ice core, the scientists from BAS learned something startling. The amount of CO_2 in our atmosphere today is 27 percent higher than it was in their samples of ancient atmosphere. And it's rising faster and faster. Inside the Dome C ice core, a slow increase in CO_2 took place over a thousand years, where it took us modern-day humans just 17 years to cause the same kind of increase.

An overview of the British Antarctic Survey camp at Dome C.

Our national parks contain natural treasures, as their names often suggest. We must all make sure there is never a place called Global Warming National Park.

National Park became even more well-known from a famous cartoon character from the 1970s called Yogi Bear, but today, grizzly bears at Yellowstone can't find food and are starving. The trees they depend on for much of their food — pine nuts and moths — are dying from an infestation of beetles that thrive in warmer weather. The Florida Everglades are losing mangrove trees, which protect the area from rising sea levels. If the growth of mangrove trees can't keep up with the increased seawater, the freshwater Everglades will disappear — and along with that, the plants and animals that live in this habitat. And there are many other national parks that

Backyard BBQ

Here's what can happen in your own backyard (or close by) as the globe starts to sizzle and CO_2 levels continue to rise.

Poison ivy grows larger and becomes itchier.

Urushiol (can you say it fast three times?) is the toxin that makes poison ivy itchy. The more carbon dioxide in the air, the more urushiol the plant produces.

Fall leaves turn a dull color and won't last as long.

Green leaves need at least one frost to trigger their color change to red. As summer heat lasts longer, sometimes through the fall months, frosts are delayed and the beautiful colors we've come to expect all over the northeastern United States are being threatened.

Ski seasons get shorter.

In some ski resorts in Oregon and Washington, there's simply too much rain and not enough snow to last a whole ski season. Did you know that the 2006 Winter Olympics in Italy had to make fake snow because there wasn't enough of the real stuff?

Allergies are triggered and asthma worsens.

Ragweed and pinecones produce much more pollen when carbon dioxide levels are higher.

Outdoor ice rinks shrink.

Ice skaters and hockey players in places like Wisconsin and Massachusetts are finding their outdoor sports are getting tougher to play, due to warmer winters that keep lakes from freezing completely and rinks from staying frozen.

Disease-carrying ticks and mosquitoes move up in the world.

As areas above the equator warm up, ticks and mosquitoes can now exist in northern places where they could not have before — bringing Lyme disease, malaria, West Nile Virus, dengue, and yellow fever from their former exotic homes.

Bark beetle population explodes.

Cold winters used to kill this pesky tree-eater, but with warmer weather, many species of trees are falling prey to them — trees that provide food for bears and other animals.

Pancakes get drier.

Maple syrup is one of New England's signature businesses, and the sugar maple trees are already feeling the effects of global warming. Since the winters aren't consistently cold, the sap flows earlier, and sugar makers tap the trees too soon. When the weather turns cold again, the flow stops, shortening the season and reducing supply dramatically.

Part 3
Extinction Stinks

Connect the Dots

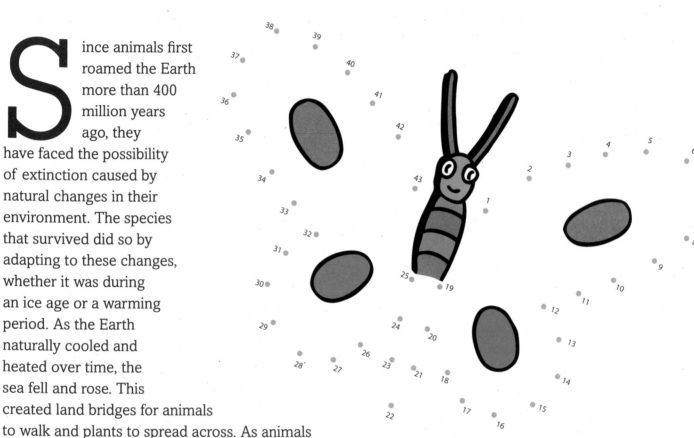

Since animals first roamed the Earth more than 400 million years ago, they have faced the possibility of extinction caused by natural changes in their environment. The species that survived did so by adapting to these changes, whether it was during an ice age or a warming period. As the Earth naturally cooled and heated over time, the sea fell and rose. This created land bridges for animals to walk and plants to spread across. As animals bumped into one another and plants invaded other plants' territories, some survived and some did not. This is a natural process and it has worked for the planet Earth for millions of years. Until today. **Right now, there are too many plants and animals becoming extinct in too short a time.** Scientists predict that in just 50 years, more than one million species will be doomed to extinction because of global warming.

Species of frogs, butterflies, penguins, and polar bears are all threatened because they cannot adapt fast enough to the changes caused by increased greenhouse gases. Whether it's a disturbed forest ecosystem or shrinking sheets of ice to stand on, animals' ability to fulfill their primary needs for survival are disappearing.

Don't Put Bleach in the Colors, Um, Corals!

If you've ever gone snorkeling or seen a picture of coral reefs, then you know the rainbow of colors that is found in these magical places under the sea. Regrettably, the colors are being bleached out of the coral — much worse than making a mistake with the laundry.

Over the past 200 years, our oceans have absorbed about half of the CO_2 emissions that are in the atmosphere from the burning of fossil fuels. That's an enormous amount, which only shows how important the oceans are to our natural carbon cycle. But the oceans also absorb excess heat and solar radiation from the atmosphere. This is making the water warmer. And unfortunately, warmer oceans are putting coral at risk, big-time.

A Tiny Snail with a Big Bite

The coral reefs of Southeast Asia are home to the amazing cone snail. This tiny crawler produces a venom so powerful, it can paralyze a small fish in seconds. But it can also help ease the pain of a very sick person. Doctors have taken the cone snail's poison and turned it into a valuable medicine that has been helping many people. Who knows how many other medical miracles hiding in the coral reefs might never even be discovered if we destroy this precious ecosystem under the sea?

Coral enjoys a **symbiotic** relationship with a certain algae called zooxanthellae (don't try to pronounce it — we can't). Symbiotic means they both get something out of the deal. Kind of like you and your best friend: You've got a large, empty lot next door. He's got the foul ball from Game 2 of the World Series. Together, you can play one fantastic game of catch.

Coral reefs give algae a safe, sunny home, and algae provide food for coral. Zooxanthellae also give coral something else in this tidy arrangement: their brilliant colors. Coral aren't that pretty on their own; it's the zooxanthellae that have bright red, orange, and brown pigments.

Bleached coral off the coast of Halfway Island in the Keppel Island Group in 2002.

When water temperatures rise, the algae cannot photosynthesize — the chemical reaction that converts sunlight and CO_2 into sugars is blocked. This results in a buildup of chemicals that poison the zooxanthellae. Scientists are still trying to figure out this next part: In an act of survival, either the coral spits out the zooxanthellae or the toxic stuff that has built up in the zooxanthellae triggers something in the coral that hurts both of them. Either way, the coral loses its source of color and turns white, almost as if it has grown old overnight. **Bleached coral becomes weaker and more vulnerable to disease, predators, and storms — not to mention becoming a pretty feeble hideout for exotic fish.** Bleached coral *can* recover, but only if cooler water temperatures return.

As if bleaching weren't bad enough, coral has something else to stress about: acidity. All liquids are either acid or alkaline, which are chemical terms for the type of molecules that make up the liquids. The terms are opposites, meaning that if you mix an alkali with an acid, the alkali neutralizes it, or takes out the parts that make it so acidic. Orange juice is acidic. Toothpaste is alkaline. (This is why orange juice tastes so weird right after you brush your teeth!) Pure water is exactly in between, or neutral. Our oceans are alkaline. If the ocean chemistry falls closer to acid by even a small amount, it can affect everything. If only all this bleaching could just leave the coral squeaky clean, instead of fighting for their lives.

Fact: Increased CO_2 in our atmosphere is making the oceans more acidic. Coral (and all shellfish) need a certain level of calcium in order to make their hard shells. But higher acidity tilts the delicate balance of calcium in the water, reducing the amount available to coral and shellfish to build their protective skeletons. With some microscopic animals, it can even dissolve their shells.

Kiss This Toad Good-bye

There are many species of amphibians at risk of extinction from global warming. One-third of them, actually. This is quite a large number. If you have two best friends, it would be like one of you moving far away. The giant glass frog, the coqui tree frog, and the harlequin frog are just some of the amphibians at risk. But none was more spectacular than the golden toad. We say "was" because the last golden toad was seen on May 15, 1989.

Discovered in 1966, the golden toad was a small creature the color of a bright orange sunset. It was found in only one place — the Monteverde Cloud Forest Preserve in Costa Rica; in only one area — the upper slopes of the mountain. **Since the golden toad had such thin, sensitive skin, this cool, moist location was probably the only place where it could thrive.** There was something else that made the golden toad rare. For most of the year it lived underground in mossy burrows and came outside only for a few days to mate. You can imagine how exciting it was when researchers actually spotted one.

So what happened to these jewels of the forest? Let's look at the weather pattern of Monteverde. Monteverde is a cloud forest, which is different from a rain forest. Most of the year, the mountaintop is

The Monteverde Cloud Forest.

covered in a foggy mist, which keeps the area cool and comfortable for the thousands of animals and plants that live there. Scientists discovered that between 1976 and 1999 there were more and more days when the clouds didn't touch the mountaintop but instead floated just above it. This happened because the Pacific Ocean became warmer, heating up the air with evaporation, making it impossible for clouds to form as low as the mountaintop.

The warm air above Monteverde was forced to rise even higher to become cool enough to condense. **Without the lower mist, the forest dried up just enough to damage the golden toad's tender skin.**

We wish this were a fairy tale and that the handsome prince of the cloud forest, the golden toad, would reappear. But alas, this story is real. And no one knows how many more amphibians will suffer the same fate.

A Fungus Among Us

New research has found that the deadly chytrid fungus could have also been responsible for the golden toad's demise. This skin fungus thrives in areas where the nighttime temperature is warmer than average — exactly the conditions brought about by global warming in Central and South America.

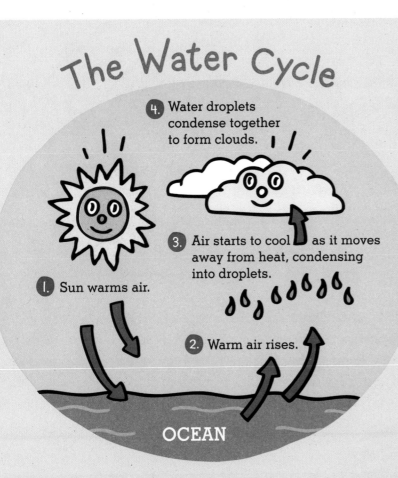

The Water Cycle

4. Water droplets condense together to form clouds.

3. Air starts to cool as it moves away from heat, condensing into droplets.

1. Sun warms air.

2. Warm air rises.

OCEAN

Up, Up, and Away

When the climate warms, plants and animals move toward the poles (north if they live in the northern half of the globe, south if they live in the southern half), seeking cooler temperatures much the same way you head to an air-conditioned mall or movie theater when the day gets too hot. But what happens to the plants and animals that already live near the poles? **Where do they go when there is nowhere else to run?**

Monarch butterfly.

Part 4
What You Can Do to Stop Global Warming

Clean Up Your Room!

I f you're like most kids, your room probably could use a little cleaning up. And if your mom's like most moms, she's probably been nagging you about it. She's right, by the way. You made the mess. You should clean it up. Well, the planet is kind of like one big messy bedroom. And guess what? The United States is making the biggest mess of all. We produce 25 percent of the world's carbon dioxide, making us the biggest polluter on the planet. So we need to play the largest part in helping to clean it up.

Mayors in cities all across America have signed an agreement to lower CO_2 emissions in their towns. The idea began in Seattle with Mayor Greg Nickels. It's called the U.S. Mayors Climate Protection Agreement, and its goal is to cut greenhouse gas emissions to levels below what they were in 1990 by 2012.

Here's what some cities have already done: Portland, Oregon, built 730 miles (1,175 km) of bike paths; Austin, Texas, gave tax breaks to homes and businesses for building green structures; Salt Lake City, Utah, converted 1,630 traffic signals to energy-efficient lightbulbs.

To find out if your mayor has already signed the agreement, check the Web site www.coolcities.us. If your city isn't listed there, then make a copy of the letter on page 73, stick it in an envelope, and send it to your mayor. If your city *is* there, do a victory dance, then find another city you've always liked and send the letter to its mayor. **The more mayors, the less CO$_2$!**

California, Here We Come!

Under the leadership of Governor Arnold Schwarzenegger, the state of California passed a landmark bill that made it the first state to limit global warming pollution. California has pledged to reduce carbon dioxide emissions to 1990 levels by the year 2020, and it also pledges to bring down levels to 80 percent below 1990 levels by the year 2050. We hope that other states across the nation will follow this example.

Cyclists take advantage of the new bike paths in Portland, Oregon.

To find out the name and address of a mayor, go to www.usmayors.org.

Dear Mayor _____,

Global warming is real and it's here to stay — unless we do something to stop it. There's an amazing agreement that more than 400 of your fellow mayors have signed. It's called the U.S. Mayors Climate Protection Agreement. It's a 12-step program that sets reasonable goals for your city to reduce carbon dioxide emissions to below what the levels were in 1990. Please join these other mayors in being leaders in the fight to stop global warming.

The kids of the world are depending on you.

Sincerely,

_____, Age_____

Or go paperless . . .

Check www.scholastic.com/downtoearthguide to download and e-mail this letter to your mayor!

How Many Concerned Kids Does It Take to Screw in a Lightbulb?

One. As long as it's a compact **fluorescent** bulb.

We think Thomas Edison would be thrilled to know that someone one-upped him by inventing a better lightbulb. It's not that his lightbulb wasn't incredible, it's just that all lightbulbs use electricity, which burns fossil fuels, which release greenhouse gases into the atmosphere and cause global warming. So why not try a bulb that uses *less* electricity and therefore releases *less* carbon dioxide?

A compact fluorescent lightbulb is 75% more energy-efficient than a regular lightbulb.

If you put a regular 60-watt **incandescent** bulb into a light you keep on most of the day, you might get 800 **lumens** for two months before it burns out. Lumens is a fancy-schmancy word for the total amount of light that a bulb is capable of generating.

With a 15-watt compact fluorescent bulb, you get 800 lumens for 20 months — ten times longer!

Compact fluorescent bulbs do the same amount of work as incandescents, yet use less energy, emit less CO_2, and last longer. It's like getting an upgrade on your iTunes software. Compact fluorescents are *new and improved* lightbulbs! If we sound like a commercial, we can't help it. This is an exciting and easy way to help stop global warming.

The reason compact fluorescent bulbs use less energy is they produce much less heat — which for a lightbulb is just wasted energy, because we only need the light. Touch a lit compact fluorescent bulb and it will feel cool.

Regular lightbulbs use four times more energy than compact fluorescent bulbs. Four times more is the equivalent of having four PlayStations instead of one. **What a waste.** You might even feel embarrassed by having so much. Similarly, we don't need all that wattage; we're using more than we need to do the job. The wasted electricity just burns more fossil fuels.

Though some compact fluorescent bulbs cost more than incandescent bulbs, you can end up saving at least 30 dollars on your family's electric bill over the life of the bulb.

Change a lightbulb today. All it takes is one person. And maybe a ladder.

A Bright Idea . . .

If every kid in America swapped one regular bulb for a compact fluorescent, we could prevent more than 30 *billion* pounds (13.6 billion kg) of greenhouse gas emissions and save enough energy to light more than 15 million homes for an entire year. It would be like taking 14 million cars off the road.

Gulp!

That's *plug* spelled backward, for all you word game experts. The reason why this page isn't called "plug" is because we want you to think about plugs differently and *un*plug your chargers. Believe it or not, leaving a charger plugged into the wall even after you remove your cell phone, iPod, GAME BOY, radio-controlled toy car, or MP3 player still drains energy. Plugged-in chargers use what's called phantom power, or standby power. In other words, it's power that you don't need and that is wasted. Just like Thomas Edison's hot lightbulb. Touch the plugged-in charger and it's warm.

Is Your Refrigerator *Running*?

The typical home contributes two times more global warming pollution than the average car. Because it is always running, the refrigerator is the single biggest energy-eating appliance in your house. To reduce your carbon footprint at home, urge your parents to buy appliances with a blue- or black-and-white ENERGY STAR sticker.

Biomass Power

Believe it or not, dead trees, yard clippings, wood chips, straw, underbrush, switch grass, and composting material can produce electricity, heat, and fuel. Before this stuff was trash, it was alive, which means it was part of the **carbon cycle**. And that means it stored energy in the form of carbon. When the plants were alive, the photosynthesis process took the sun's energy and converted it to carbohydrates. That energy is recaptured when biomass is burned in huge boilers. The heat released from this process is used to turn water into steam, which turns a steam turbine to create electricity. Recent discoveries have even found a way to convert leaves and plant stalks into the alternative fuel ethanol.

If we used just one-eighth of what the world produces in biomass each year, it would provide all the energy needs of every single person on the planet.

There is no single solution. In fact, we need *every* solution. The future holds even more solutions, and you'll be a part of that.

93

What Do You Want to Be When You Grow Up?

A Sustainable Career

If something is sustainable, it will last and never be depleted. Your love for your pet is sustainable, even though your cat might pee on your bedspread or your dog might chew your favorite flip-flops. Bamboo, a quick-growing grass that is planted just for the purpose of constructing furniture and floors, is sustainable. Wind and solar power are sustainable.

It's never too early to dream about what you want to be when you grow up. Here are a few careers that you might want to think about:

Forest Resource Officer

Promotes respect for the web of life in a forest ecosystem. Takes action to protect the biodiversity of forests and selects species for reforestation. Can work in national parks, universities, or recycled-paper mills.

Glacial Geologist

Focuses on the Earth's past and present as it relates to the physical properties and movement of glaciers and ice sheets. Discovers how glaciers were formed and what has happened to them since their formation. Can work as a university professor or in an engineering firm.

Hydrologist

Studies the physical properties of underground and surface water. Examines rain — its rate of infiltration into the soil, its movement through the Earth, and its return to the ocean and atmosphere. Studies flood control and groundwater contamination issues. Can work as an environmental consultant in an architectural firm or for the Department of Defense.

Environmental Communicator

Gathers support to protect threatened ecosystems. Informs people about crucial environmental issues through newspaper or magazine stories, Web sites, videos, films, and photographs that show sustainable living and showcase nature. Can work for the government, in radio or television, or at museums.

Agricultural Technologist

Helps farmers with planning, cultivating, harvesting, and storing crops. Demonstrates environmentally sustainable farming techniques and suggests what crops to grow in particular soils and growing conditions. Can work in a small village or a big city.

Wind Development Associate

Helps with the construction of wind farms. Analyzes wind, sites, and environmental data. Can work at either a wind farm or a corporate office.

A career in the environmental field is sustainable because, in the future, we will need more and more experts who understand global warming.

Biofuels Engineer

Produces renewable fuels such as biodiesel, biomass, ethanol, and biogas. Can work at a biofuel plant and travel to farms where seed crops are grown.

Solar Sales Representative

Designs solar power systems for homes or businesses and convinces people to switch to solar power. Can work for a solar energy firm but can also do some work from home.

Atmospheric Scientist, or Meteorologist

Predicts the weather. Identifies climate trends by studying past and present weather. Studies air pressure, temperature, humidity, and wind speed. Can work for the government at weather stations or in broadcasting.

There are so many wonderful careers in the environmental field that it would have taken 20 more pages to list them all. We didn't think we could "sustain" your interest for that long.

Live for Today, but Protect the Future

Former Norwegian prime minister Gro Harlem Brundtland is credited with introducing the groundbreaking concept of "sustainable development" onto the world stage. The idea is that everyone — businesspeople, politicians, farmers, doctors, lawyers, environmentalists, parents, and schoolchildren, too — is responsible for creating a healthy and happy world today that will ensure the ability of future generations to meet their own needs for a healthy and happy tomorrow.

What Else You Can Do

Let Your Fingers Do the Marching

In August 1963, when Martin Luther King, Jr., led the March on Washington, 250,000 people marched along with him in support of civil rights for blacks and minorities. It was the largest demonstration ever held in the U.S. capital. In April 1970, millions turned up in cities all over the United States for the first celebration of Earth Day. In fact, the Earth Day events led to the passage of two landmark laws, the Clean Air Act and the Endangered Species Act, as well as the formation of the Environmental Protection Agency (EPA).

The thing about marches is that they generally last only one day. But now there's a way to march to stop global warming every day. It's called a virtual march and it's as easy to do as browsing and clicking. **The idea is to get as many people as possible to use the Internet instead of the pavement to register their concern for the environment. The message you'll be telling our leaders is that we want solutions to global warming. Now.**

Go to www.stopglobalwarming.org. When you see some of the other folks who are marching virtually, you'll know what good company you're in.

C. C. + S.

It's not someone's initials on the bathroom wall. It stands for Carbon Capture and Storage, and the name says it all. This is a way to prevent carbon dioxide emissions from getting into our atmosphere in the first place. Here are just two areas in which energy companies are currently doing research:

1. Capturing CO_2 from the smokestacks of power plants and feeding it to a hothouse of hungry algae.

2. Burying CO_2 deep in the ground by pumping it from the power plant directly into old oil and natural gas fields.

Carbon Capture and Storage is an exciting solution. And it lasts a lot longer than a school crush.

Go Carbon Neutral

The band Coldplay went a step further than marching. They made their carbon footprint disappear. Making an album uses up a lot of energy, from running the recording studio to producing all of those CD jewel boxes to driving the trucks and planes that have to get them to the stores. After they cut their CD *A Rush of Blood to the Head*, Coldplay bought 10,000 mango trees for villagers in Karnataka, India. The idea is that the trees will provide a carbon sink for all the CO_2 the band emitted in making and selling its CD. Of course, we can't plant enough trees to absorb all the CO_2 released from the amount of fossil fuels we are burning now, but it's one of the many things we can do.

There are many companies that can help a rock band — or a family — go carbon neutral. Here are two of them: www.carbonfund.org and www.nativeenergy.com.

Come Up with the Next Great Idea

You never know who or where a solution will come from. A ski resort in Andermatt, Switzerland, figured that since their glacier was melting, they'd protect it from heat, solar energy, and rain. They covered the whole glacier, an area more than 32,300 square feet (3,000 m²) wide, with insulating foam — kind of like putting the glacier in a giant thermos. It cost a bundle, but the insulation can be reused after every ski season.

A company called Simple Shoes recycles car tires and plastic milk jugs to make shoes for both kids and adults, saving the energy it would take if they made shoes from new rubber and plastic. Their shoes also contain materials from other renewable sources like cork trees and jute bushes, which don't require the cutting of old-growth trees to get at the stuff inside. The flip-flops even make tire-tread marks when you walk on the beach!

Kenny Luna, an eighth-grade teacher in New York, challenged everyone in his school and the surrounding community to change one lightbulb to a compact fluorescent bulb and even got Home Depot to donate the bulbs.

Anne Lasker, an elementary school parent in Los Angeles, started a Trashion Show, where kids make their outfits out of recycled material.

And an eighth-grade boy in California made a CD of original songs that he wrote and recorded at home on his computer. He then sold the CDs at school and donated the money to a stop global warming cause.

Become a Global Warming Activist

We hope you will become a global warming activist. If you can change the way you think, you can help others change the way they think. If you can make one small change in your actions, like unplugging a charger from the wall, then you'll set an example for others to do it, too. **We need big, bold ideas for this global problem.** So let's all get down to Earth and start thinking. No idea is too outrageous. No solution is too far from possibility. Will you be the one to come up with a new solution?

The Earth is depending on you!

Words To Know

albedo effect
The amount of light a body or surface reflects and the amount of light that is absorbed.

carbon cycle
The process in the ecosystem by which carbon is exchanged among organisms, oceans, atmosphere, and land.

carbon footprint
A measure of the amount of carbon dioxide a business or individual emits through the burning of fossil fuels.

carbon sink
An area of the Earth that permanently removes carbon dioxide from the atmosphere and binds it in organic compounds. The most important carbon sinks are the world's oceans and forests.

circumpolar
Wind, ocean currents, stars, animals, people — anything that moves around either pole of the Earth.

clear-cutting
The cutting or harvesting of all of the trees in an area at one time with no plan for regenerating or renewing the forest.

equilibrium
A state of balance kept between opposing forces or elements so that no change occurs.

fluorescent
A lamp in which a phosphor coating transforms ultraviolet energy into visible light. Uses far less electrical energy than an incandescent lamp.

fossil fuel
The remains of prehistoric plant and animal life, such as coal, oil, and natural gas, that are used to provide energy when burned.

global warming
An increase in the Earth's average temperature that causes changes in climate patterns worldwide.

green
Also known as "going green"; the adoption of a sustainable lifestyle that respects the environment while actively working to curb our carbon footprint and leave the world better than we found it.

greenhouse gas

A heat-trapping gas in the Earth's atmosphere that is also released from the burning of fossil fuels.

incandescent

A common form of artificial light in which a filament contained in a vacuum is heated to brightness by an electric current. Only 5 percent of the energy output of incandescent lighting is light, while the remaining 95 percent is heat.

long-wave energy

Energy that leaves the Earth by being radiated from the surface back into the atmosphere.

lumen

A unit of measurement quantifying the amount of light emitted from a light source.

organism

Any individual living creature, made of either one cell or multiple cells.

permafrost

A layer of soil below the Earth's surface where the temperature has remained below freezing for two or more years.

polar ice cap

The permanent mass of sea ice that forms a jagged circle around the North Pole, and that covers about 70 percent of the Arctic Ocean.

sediment

A material, deposited by wind, water, or glaciers, that sinks to the bottom of a body of water.

short-wave energy

The light energy that comes directly from the sun.

stratification

The physical layering of ocean water resulting from density differences caused by salt or temperature variations.

symbiotic

A close and prolonged relationship between two or more different kinds of organisms in which both benefit.

water vapor

The water present in the atmosphere in a gaseous form.

Suggestions for Further Reading

Braasch, Gary. *Earth under Fire: How Global Warming Is Changing the World.* Berkeley, Ca.: University of California Press, 2007.

Gore, Al. *An Inconvenient Truth: The Crisis of Global Warming.* New York: Viking Children's Books, 2007.

Langley, Andrew. *Hurricanes, Tsunamis and Other Natural Disasters.* Boston: Kingfisher, 2006.

Revkin, Andrew. *The North Pole Was Here: Puzzles & Perils at the Top of the World.* Boston: Kingfisher, 2006.

Sussman, Art, Ph.D. *Dr. Art's Guide to Planet Earth.* White River Junction, Vt.: Chelsea Green, 2000.

———. *Dr. Art's Guide to Science.* Hoboken, N.J.: Jossey Bass, 2006.

Taylor, Barbara. *How to Save the Planet.* New York: Franklin Watts, 2000.

Vogel, Carole Garbuny. *Human Impact (The Restless Sea).* New York: Franklin Watts, 2003.

Cool Web Sites to Check Out

adventureecology.com
Here's an interactive game that lets you travel the world as an eco-adventurer to find global warming hot spots.

planetfriendly.com
This Web site certifies products, places, and processes that help the planet instead of harming it. One of the things you'll discover is plates, cups, straws, and other food containers made from corn. Look for them at the food court in your mall and at supermarket salad bars.

stopglobalwarming.org

You can sign up here for the virtual march and also order the coolest accessories around: leather bracelets that say STOP GLOBAL WARMING and flip-flops that have the Stop Global Warming logo on the straps.

stopglobalwarming.msn.com
On this MSN Web site, you can get up-to-the-minute global warming news and energy saving tips, and watch videos or read interviews of your favorite athletes, musicians, and actors talking about global warming. Windows Live Spaces will also help you create your own blog about global warming.

nrdc.org
This is the official Web site for the Natural Resources Defense Council, one of the world's best watchdogs for our environment. Click on "Kids Make Waves" to learn all about the many ways you can help.

scholastic.com/ downtoearthguide
This Web site will provide even more down-to-Earth facts and background information on this book, including downloadables, e-cards, and more.

Source Notes

Authors' Note

Page x *The third installment of IPCC's four-part report* . . . : IPCC, 2007: Climate Change 2007: The Physical Science Basis. Contribution of Working Group I to the Fourth Assessment Report of the Intergovernmental Panel on Climate Change [Solomon, S., D. Qin, M. Manning, Z. Chen, M. Marquis, K. B. Avery, M. Tignor and H. L. Miller (eds.)]. Cambridge University Press, Cambridge, United Kingdom and New York, NY, USA.

Page x *the Stern Report, issued in England* . . . : Stern, N., et al. *The Economics of Climate Change: The Stern Review.* HM Treasury: London, 2006. Accessed online May 9, 2007, at http://www.hm-treasury.gov.uk/independent_reviews/stern_review_economics_climate_change/sternreview_index.cfm.

Page x *Scientists at the National* . . . : Stroeve, J., et al. "Arctic sea ice decline: Faster than forecast." *Geophysical Research Letters,* Vol. 34, L09501, doi:10.1029/2007GL029703 (2007).

Page x *China is expected* . . . : Bradsher, Keith. "China to Pass U.S. in 2009 in Emissions." *The New York Times* 7 November 2006; Collier, Robert. "A Warming World: China about to pass U.S. as world's top generator of greenhouse gases." *San Francisco Chronicle* 5 March 2007.

Page xi *Australia and Canada* . . . : "Canada to ban incandescent lightbulbs by 2012." *Reuters* 25 April 2007.

Page xi *The city of San Francisco* . . . : Goodyear, Charlie. "S.F. First City to Ban Plastic Shopping Bags." *San Francisco Chronicle* 28 March 2007.

Page xi *including Home Depot* . . . : *Sierra Magazine* May/June 2007, p. 33.

Part One: It's Getting Hot in Here

Page 2 *Carbon dioxide is released* . . . : E-mail correspondence with Dr. Susan Hassol, climate analyst and author.

Page 3 *Cars, factories, and electric power plants* . . . : www.fueleconomy.com.

Page 3 *global warming is causing* . . . : Tebaldi, Claudia, et al. "Going to the Extremes: An Intercomparison of Model-Simulated Historical and Future Changes in Extreme Events." *Climatic Change* 79.3/4 (2006): 185–211.

Page 3 *Global warming is also causing less snow* . . . : Stauth, David. "Global Warming Poses Risk to Pacific Northwest Snowpack, Ski Resorts." *Oregon State University News and Communications Services* 7 March 2006.

Page 4 *Both glass-covered greenhouses* . . . : Interview with John Steelman, Campaign Director, Natural Resources Defense Council Climate Center.

Page 7 *Maybe an earthquake* . . . : Interview with John Steelman, Campaign Director, Natural Resources Defense Council Climate Center.

Page 7 *Where does all this CO_2 Come From?*: CO_2 emissions by end-use sector, Energy Information Administration, 2004; Emissions of greenhouse gases in the US 2004, Report #DOE/EIA-0573(2004); US Emissions Inventory 2006, Environmental Protection Agency, ESEPA #430-R-06-002.

Page 13 *Keeling Curve graph*: Flannery, Tim. *The Weather Makers.* New York: Atlantic Monthly Press, 2005, p. 25.

Page 15 *One tree can absorb the amount of CO_2* . . . : Shropshire, David E. *Global Climate Change.* Idaho National Engineering & Environmental Laboratory, July 2002.

Page 16 *Inside the Dome C ice core* . . . : E-mail correspondence with Eric Wolff, British Antarctic Survey.

Page 16 *The amount of CO_2 in our atmosphere today is at 27 percent higher* . . . : E-mail correspondence with Dr. Susan Hassol, climate analyst and author.

Page 18 *You can see this relationship for yourself* . . . : Siegenthaler, Urs, et al. "Stable Carbon Cycle-Climate Relationship During the Late Pleistocene." *Science* 310 (2005): 1313–1317.

Page 18 *Well, the Earth's average temperature* . . . : EPA Climate Change, Basic Information. http://epa.gov/climatechange/basicinfo.html.

Page 19 *Eleven out of twelve of the years* . . . : IPCC AR4 WG1 Summary for Policymakers, p. 5.

Page 19 *July 2005 to June 2006* . . . : National Climatic Data Center (NCDC). www.ncdc.noaa.gov/oa/climate/research/2006/jul/jul06.html.

Page 20 *Well, one degree hotter for the world on average* . . . : IPCC AR4 WG1, p. 5.

Page 20 *Warm, westerly winds* . . . : E-mail correspondence with Dr. Gareth Marshall, climatologist for the British Antarctic Survey.

Page 22 *Something that is not a source* . . . : Interview with John Steelman, Campaign Director, Natural Resources Defense Council Climate Center.

Page 22 *Over forty years, one acre* . . . : Shropshire, David E. *Global Climate Change.* Idaho National Engineering & Environmental Laboratory, July 2002.

Page 22 *6.6 billion*: World Population Clock, http://www.census.gov/main/www/popclock.html.

Page 22 *Every two seconds* . . . : Greenpeace. "The Amazon's Major Threat: Illegal logging." Press report July 2000.

Page 23 *the fire season has become two months longer:* Westerling, A. L. "Warming and Earlier Spring Increase Western U.S. Forest Wildfire Activity." *Science* 313 (2006): 940–943.

Page 23 *Forests and soils store carbon dioxide* . . . : Conversation with Nigel Pervis, The Nature Conservancy.

Page 24 *The problem now is that with so much CO_2* . . . : Correspondence with Daniel A. Lashof, Ph.D., Science Director, Natural Resources Defense Council Climate Center.

Page 24 *It has to do not only* . . . : Interview with Joel Reynolds, Director, Natural Resources Defense Council Marine Mammal Protection Program.

Page 25 *If CO$_2$ emissions continue to rise* . . . : Correspondence with Dr. Susan Hassol, climate analyst and author.

Page 26 *The average American adult* . . . : IPCC AR4 WGI, SPM, p. 3.

Page 26 *It's an amount that scientists* . . . : Interview with Tim Greeff, Campaign Director, Natural Resources Defense Council Climate Center.

Page 27 *Using a screensaver* . . . : Correspondence with Noah Horowitz, Senior Scientist, Natural Resources Defense Council; http://www.energystar.gov/index.cfm?c=energy_awareness.bus_energy_use for conversions.

Page 27 *Turning on the lights* . . . : Energy Information Agency, Department of Energy, www.eia.doe.gov.

Page 27 *Taking a bath* . . . : The number is based on a flow rate of 5 gallons per minute into a tub filling in 4 minutes and heating 20 gallons of water, then converting Btu to therms to kWh to pounds of CO$_2$. Ibid; www.showerheadsrus.com/sp-bin/spirit?page=24&CATALOG=5.

Page 27 *Riding in a car* . . . *(based on driving to school 2.5 miles each way)*: The median distance to school for children ages 5–15 years, http://www.cdc.gov/mmwr/preview/mmwrhtml/mm5132al.htm.

Page 27 *. . . in a car that gets 20 miles per gallon*: Conversation with Tim Greeff, Campaign Director, Natural Resources Defense Council Climate Center, for conversions of mpg to lbs of CO$_2$.

Page 27 *Now, if you take* . . . : U.S. Census Bureau, 2000 Census.

Page 27 *Because CO$_2$ stays in the atmosphere* . . . : IPCC AR4 WGI, p. 11, "Scientific Assessment of Ozone Depletion," 10.21.

Part Two: Weird, Wacky Weather

Page 35 *But overall, rainfall is increasing* . . . : Climate Change 2001, Figure 15. Robert T. Watson, Chair, Intergovernmental Panel on Climate Change, at the resumed Sixth Conference of parties to the United Nations Framework Convention on Climate Change. 19 July 2001.

Page 37 *as the temperature gets cooler* . . . : Interview with John Steelman, Campaign Director, Natural Resources Defense Council Climate Center.

Page 37 *While it is true* . . . : E-mail correspondence with Dr. Heidi Cullen, The Weather Channel climate expert and host of *The Climate Code*.

Page 37 *In the year 2000* . . . : "Natural disasters at record level in 2000." *Reuters* 29 December 2000.

Page 37 *Even in Asia* . . . : International Monetary Fund. "Picture This: Hit by Disaster." *Finance & Development* 40.3 (2003).

Page 37 *The pools of standing water* . . . : www.westnile.ca.gov/mosquito_control.html.

Page 38 *But with warmer temperatures caused by global warming* . . . : Correspondence with Dr. Susan Hassol, climate analyst and author.

Page 39 *Here are the areas* . . . : NCDC. www.ncdc.noaa.gov/oa/climate/research/2006/jul/us-drought.html.

Page 43 *And 2007 is expected* . . . : www.abcnews.go.com/us/Globalwarming/wirestory?id=2769263.

Page 44 *Already in the last 100 years* . . . : IPCC TAR WG1 SPM, p. 4.

Page 44 *Half of it* . . . : EPA, Climate Change Science, "Sea Level Changes," http://www.epa.gov/climatechange/science/recentslc.html.

Page 44 *climatologists are most worried about the Greenland ice sheet*: "L.A. Times Special Report: Greenland's Ice Sheet is Slip-Sliding Away." *Los Angeles Times* 25 June 2006.

Page 45 *If the Greenland ice sheet melts completely* . . . : "L.A. Times Special Report: Greenland's Ice Sheet is Slip-Sliding Away." *Los Angeles Times* 25 June 2006; IPCC AR4.

Page 46 *But scientists are predicting that within 25 years* . . . : Yohe, Evelyne. "Sizing up the Earth's Glaciers." NASA Earth Science Enterprise Data and Services, National Snow and Ice Data Center DAAC, 22 June 2004.

Page 48 *Poison Ivy* . . . : Mohan, Jacqueline E., et al. "Biomass and Toxicity Responses of Poison Ivy to Elevated Atmospheric CO$_2$." *PNAS* 103.24 (2006): 9086–9089.

Page 48 *Fall leaves* . . . : New England Regional Assessment Group. *Preparing for a Changing Climate: The Potential Consequences of Climate Variability and Change*. New England Regional Overview, U.S. Global Change Research Program. University of New Hampshire, 2001.

Page 48 *Ski seasons get shorter*: Hecox, Walter E., et al, eds. *The 2005 Colorado College State of the Rockies Report Card*. Colorado Springs, Colorado: The Colorado College State of the Rockies Project, 2005.

Page 49 *Allergies are triggered and asthma worsens*: Ziska, L. H., et al. "Cities as harbingers of climate change: common ragweed, urbanization and public health." *Journal of Allergy Clinical Immunology* 111.2 (2003): 290–295.

Page 49 *Outdoor ice rinks shrink*: Correspondence with Eric Chivian, M.D., Director, Center for Health and the Global Environment, Harvard Medical School.

Page 49 *Disease-carrying ticks and mosquitoes* . . . : Patz, Jonathan, et al. "Impact of Regional Climate Change on Human Health." *Nature* 438.7066 (2005): 310–317.

Page 49 *ticks and mosquitoes can now exist* . . . : E. Lindgren, L. Tälleklint, and T. Polfeldt. "Impact of climatic change on the northern latitude limit and population density of the disease-transmitting European Tick, *Ixodes ricinus*." *Environmental Health Perspectives* 108.2 (2000): 119–23.

Page 49 *Bark beetle population explodes*: Juday, Glenn. "Chapter 14: Forests, land management and agriculture" in *Arctic Climate Impact Assessment, Scientific Report*. New York: Cambridge University Press, 2005.

Page 49 *Pancakes get drier*: Correspondence with Eric Chivian, M.D., Director, Center for Health and the Global Environment, Harvard Medical School.

Part Three: Extinction Stinks

Page 52 *Scientists predict that in just 50 years . . .* : "China Gets Dutch Help to Fight Floods, Droughts." *Reuters* 11 April 2007, http://www.planetark.com/avantgo/dailynewsstory.cfm?newsid=41333; "UN warns world on Africa drought." *BBC News* 23 February 2006, http://news.bbc.co.uk/2/hi/africa/4744812.stm; Marks, Kathy. "Australia's epic drought: The situation is grim." *The Independent, UK* April 2007; U.S. Drought Monitor, as of April 2007, http://www.drought.unl.edu/dm/monitor.html.

Page 57 *And it happens to eat . . .* : Interview with Joel Reynolds, Director, Natural Resources Defense Council Marine Mammal Protection Program.

Page 59 *Over the past 200 years or so . . .* : "Ocean Acidification Due to Increasing Atmospheric Carbon Dioxide." *The Royal Society* 30 June 2005.

Page 61 *Bleached coral can recover . . .* : E-mail correspondence with Dr. Susan Hassol, climate analyst and author.

Page 61 *Coral (and all shellfish) . . .* : E-mail correspondence with Dr. Susan Hassol, climate analyst and author.

Page 62 *One-third of them, actually*: Pounds, Alan, et al. "Widespread Amphibian Extinctions from Epidemic Disease Driven by Global Warming." *Nature* 439.7073 (2006): 161–167; Thomas, Chris D., et al. "Extinction Risk from Climate Change." *Nature* 427.6970 (2004): 145–147.

Page 62 *For most of the year . . .* : Flannery, Tim. *The Weather Makers.* New York: Atlantic Monthly Press, 2005, pp.115–19.

Page 63 *Scientists discovered that . . .* : Flannery, Tim. *The Weather Makers.* New York: Atlantic Monthly Press, 2005, pp.115–19.

Page 63 *New research has found that the deadly chytrid fungus . . .* : Pounds, A. & Savage, J. 2004. *Bufo periglenes.* In: IUCN 2006. *2006 IUCN Red List of Threatened Species.* www.iucnredlist.org.

Page 64 *When the climate warms, plants and animals move . . .* : Correspondence with Dr. Susan Hassol, climate analyst and author.

Page 65 *The butterflies that disappeared couldn't survive . . .* : Fox, Richard. Butterfly Conservation Initiative. *Climate Change and Habitat Loss Hit Northern Butterflies.*; Franco, Aldina M. A., et al. "Impacts of Climate Warming and Habitat Loss on Extinctions at Species' Low-latitude Range Boundaries." *Global Change Biology* 12.8 (2006): 1545–53.

Page 66 *The red squirrel is literally being pushed . . .* : Egan, Timothy. "Heat Invades Cool Heights Over Arizona Desert." *The New York Times* 27 March 2007.

Page 67 Some *stronger butterflies . . .* : E-mail correspondence with Richard Fox, Surveys Manager, Butterfly Conservation Initiative.

Part Four: What You Can Do to Stop Global Warming

Page 70 *. . . the mayors of 418 cities:* www.sierraclub.org/coolcities.

Page 75 *If every kid in America . . .* : www.energystar.gov.

Page 75 *It would be like . . .* : www.energystar.gov/ia/partners/promotions/change_light/downloads/MayorToolkit.pdf.

Page 77 *Up to 10 percent . . .* : www.eia.doe.gov.

Page 78 *Americans use ten billion . . .* : American Forest and Paper Association. www.reusablebags.com/facts.php.

Page 80 *The more trees . . .* : Natural Resources Defense Council (NRDC). "Fact Sheet: Saving Paper in School."

Page 81 *Bringing in your own . . .* : Environmental Defense Fund.

Page 81 *Last year, one major . . .* : NRDC. *Nature's Voice.*

Page 81 *You want to buy . . .* : NRDC. "Environmentally Preferable Paper: Why and How to Buy It."

Page 81 *Forty percent of the fiber . . .* : Food and Agriculture Organization, FAOSTAT.

Page 81 *Fifteen trees are cut down . . .* : Conservatree. "Trees Into Paper." 2006. www.conservatree.com/learn/EnviroIssues/TreeStats.shtml.

Page 82 *Cars that sit . . .* : U.S. Environmental Protection Agency, Office of Mobile Sources: Fact Sheet OMS-18. "Your Car and Clean Air: What YOU Can Do to Reduce Pollution." August 1994. http://www.epa.gov/otaq/consumer/18-youdo.pdf.

Page 83 *The students of the University of Washington . . .* : Organic Consumers Association. www.organicconsumers.org/2006/article 1797.cfm.

Page 86 *A hybrid is high tech . . .* : NRDC. "Clean Air and Energy."

Page 87 *When combined with regular gasoline . . .* : "Waste-to-Energy Innovation." *WE Energies.* http://www.we-energies.com/environment/renewable_energy_biomass_tinedale.htm.

Page 88 *The Indy 500 . . .* : www.indy500.com/news/story.php?story_id=4105.

Page 88 *An engine running on ethanol . . .* : Jones, Roland. "The Driver's Seat: Ethanol Boosters Hoping for Indy 500 Win." *MSNBC.* 28 May 2006. www.msnbc.msn.com/id/12740848.

Page 89 *Today, a typical wind turbine . . .* : Renewable Energy Systems. www.res-ltd.com/wind-power/faqs.htm.

Page 93 *Recent discoveries . . .* : Woodyard, Chris. "Honda Sees Possible Ethanol Breakthrough—New Microorganism Improves Efficiency." *USA Today* 15 September 2006.

Page 98 *The band Coldplay . . .* : Kher, Unmesh, et al. "How to Seize the Initiative." *Time* 3 April 2006, p. 46.

Page 99 *A company called Simple . . .* : Simple Shoe Company, "a nice little shoe company," www.simpleshoes.com, "Greentoeology," Spring 2007.

Page 99 *Kenny Luna . . .* : E-mail correspondence with Kenny Luna, eighth-grade teacher, at www.thebrightidea.blogspot.com.

Page 99 *Anne Lasker . . .* : Conversation with Anne Lasker, parent and creator of Trashion Show.

Selected Bibliography

Books

Dauncey, Guy, with Patrick Mazza. *Stormy Weather: 101 Solutions to Global Climate Change*. Gabriola Island, British Columbia, Canada: New Society Publishers, 2001.

Flannery, Tim. *The Weather Makers*. New York: Atlantic Monthly Press, 2005.

Gelbspan, Ross. *Boiling Point: How Politicians, Big Oil and Coal, Journalists and Activists Are Fueling the Climate Crisis—and What We Can Do to Avert Disaster*. New York: Basic Books, 2004.

Gore, Al. *An Inconvenient Truth*. New York: Rodale, 2006.

———. *Earth in the Balance: Ecology and the Human Spirit*. Boston: Houghton Mifflin, 2000.

Kolbert, Elizabeth. *Field Notes from a Catastrophe*. New York: Bloomsbury, 2006.

Tennesen, Michael. *The Complete Idiot's Guide to Global Warming*. New York: Alpha Publishing, 2004.

Tickell, Josh. *Biodiesel America: How to Achieve Energy Security, Free America from Middle-East Oil Dependence and Make Money Growing Fuel*. USA: Yorkshire Press, 2006.

Trask, Crissy. *It's Easy Being Green*. Layton, Utah: Gibbs Smith, 2006.

Magazines

BusinessWeek, Global Warming Issue, 16 August 2004.

The Economist, The Heat Is On Issue, September 9–15, 2006.

Mother Jones, As the World Burns Issue, June 2005.

National Geographic, Signs from Earth Issue, September 2004.

Natural History, Cooking the Climate with Coal Issue, May 2006.

Newsweek, Save the Planet — Or Else, 16 April 2007.

onearth, Natural Resources Defense Council magazine, various issues.

Time, Special Report: Global Warming Issue, 3 April 2006.

Time, The Global Warming Survival Guide, 9 April 2007.

Vanity Fair, Green Issue, May 2006.

Vanity Fair, Second Annual Green Issue, May 2007.

Articles and Reports

American Wind Energy Association. "Fact Sheet: Wind Power Today." 2004.

www.awea.org

Atkinson, Angus, et al. "Long-Term Decline in Antarctic Krill Stock and Increase in Salps Within the Southern Ocean." *Nature* 432.7013 (2004): 100–103.

Augustin, L. "New Evidence Extends Greenhouse Gas Record from Ice Cores by 50 Percent, Adding 210,000 Years." *Science* 25 November 2005.

Australian Academy of Science. "Biomass—the growing energy resource." www.science.org.au/nova/039.

Avant, Bill. "Paper or Plastic? A Simple Question, Right? Wrong!" *The Tennessee Conservationist*. January/February 2006. www.tn.gov/environment/tn_consv/archive/paperplastic.pdf.

British Antarctic Survey. *Oldest Antarctic Ice Core Reveals Climate History*. 09 June 2004 PR No. 7/2004.

Bryant, Dirk, et al. *The Last Frontier Forests: Ecosystems and economies on the edge*. Washington, D.C.: World Resources Institute, 1997.

Carey, John. "Business on a Warmer Planet." *BusinessWeek* 17 July 2006.

CNN: Science and Space, Associated Press. "Study: Earth Hottest in 400 years." 22 June 2006.

Connor, Steve. "Warmer Seas Will Wipe Out Plankton, Source of Ocean Life." *Independent News UK* 19 January 2006.

Conservatree. "Trees Into Paper." 2006. www.conservatree.com/learn/EnviroIssues/TreeStats.shtml.

Egan, Timothy. "Heat Invades Cool Heights Over Arizona Desert." *The New York Times* 27 March 2007.

Energy Information Administration. *Emissions of Greenhouse Gases in the United States, 2004*. Report #DOE/EIA 0573 (2004), December 2005.

Energy Quest. "Chapter 8: Fossil Fuels." http://www.energyquest.ca.gov/story/chapter08.html.

———. "Chapter 10: Biomass Energy." http://www.energyquest.ca.gov/story/chapter10.html.

———. "Chapter 11: Geothermal Energy." http://www.energyquest.ca.gov/story/chapter11.html.

———. "Chapter 12: Hydro Power." http://www.energyquest.ca.gov/story/chapter12.html.

Fox, Richard. Butterfly Conservation Initiative. *Climate Change and Habitat Loss Hit Northern Butterflies*.

Franco, Aldina M. A., et al. "Impacts of Climate Warming and Habitat Loss on Extinctions at Species' Low-latitude Range Boundaries." *Global Change Biology* 12.8 (2006): 1545–1553.

Heinz Center for Science, Economics, and the Environment. *Human Links to Coastal Disasters*. 2002.

Henne, Gudrun, and Christoph Thies. "Will the Last of the Ancient Forests Survive in 2050?" *Unasylva* 52.1 (2001).

"How Do Clouds Form?" *Forecasting the Weather Using Clouds*. 2001. http://snrs.unl.edu/amet351/noehrenberg/cloudformation.html.

Huisman, Jef, et al. Letter. "Reduced Mixing Generates Oscillations and Chaos in the Oceanic Deep Chlorophyll Maximum." *Nature* 439.4074 (2006): 322–325.

Intergovernmental Panel on Climate Change (IPCC). *Third Assessment Report: Climate Change 2001*.

———. *Fourth Assessment Report: Climate Change 2007: Summary for Policy Makers*.

Interstate Renewable Energy Council (IREC). *Schools Going Solar*. www.irecusa.org.

Jones, Roland. "The Driver's Seat: Ethanol Boosters Hoping for Indy 500 Win." *MSNBC*. 28 May 2006. www.msnbc.msn.com/id/12740848.

Kher, Unmesh, et al. "How to Seize the Initiative." *Time* 3 April 2006.

Malakunas, Karl. "Typhoon Saomai Kills Scores in China." *Discovery Channel: Discovery News*. 11 August 2006. http://dsc.discovery.com/news/2006/08/10/typhoon_pla.html?category=travel&guid=20060810100030.

Malcolm, Jay R., et al. "Global Warming and Extinctions of Endemic Species from Biodiversity Hotspots." *Conservation Biology* 20.2 (2006): 538–548.

Marshall, Gareth, et al. "The Impact of a Changing Southern Hemisphere Annular Mode on Antarctic Peninsula Summer Temperatures." *Journal of Climate* 19.20 (2006): 5388–5404.

McFarling, Usha Lee. "Altered Oceans: A Chemical Imbalance." *Los Angeles Times* 3 August 2006.

McGahee, Alvin L. National Oceanic Atmospheric Administration: National Climate Data Center (NCDC), United States Department of Commerce. *Selected U.S. City and State Extremes for July 2006*.

Mohan, Jacqueline E., et al. "Biomass and Toxicity Responses of Poison Ivy to Elevated Atmospheric CO_2." *PNAS* 103.24 (2006): 9086–9089.

"NASA Survey Confirms Climate Warming Impact on Polar Ice Sheets: Release 06–089." National Aeronautic and Space Administration. 8 March 2006. http://www.nasa.gov/home/hqnews/2006/mar/HQ_06089_polar_ice_sheets_melting.html.

"National Assessment of Coastal Vulnerability to Future Sea Level Rise: Report Number 076-00." *U.S. Geological Survey.* June 2000. http://pubs.usgs.gov/fs/fs76-00/fs076-00.pdf.

Natural Resources Defense Council. "Hybrid Values." www.nrdc.org/air/transportation/ghybrid.asp.

——. "Environmentally Preferable Paper: Why and How to Buy It." *Paper Industry Reform Project,* January 2005.

——. "Fact Sheet: Saving Paper in School." www.nrdc.org/greensquad/library/paper.html.

——. *Nature's Voice.* January/February 2005.

New England Regional Assessment Group. *Preparing for a Changing Climate: The Potential Consequences of Climate Variability and Change.* New England Regional Overview, U.S. Global Change Research Program. University of New Hampshire, 2001.

"Ocean Acidification Due to Increasing Atmospheric Carbon Dioxide." *The Royal Society.* 30 June 2005.

Patz, Jonathan, et al. "Impact of Regional Climate Change on Human Health." *Nature* 438.7066 (2005): 310–317.

Pounds, Alan, et al. "Widespread Amphibian Extinctions from Epidemic Disease Driven by Global Warming." *Nature* 439.7073 (2006): 161–167.

Ruttimann, Jacqueline. "Oceanography: Sick Seas." *Nature* 442.7106 (2006): 978–980.

Santer, B. D., et al. "Forced and Unforced Ocean Temperature Changes in Atlantic and Pacific Tropical Cyclogenesis Regions. *PNAS* 103.38 (2006): 13905–13910.

Saunders, Stephen, et al. "Losing Ground—Western National Parks Endangered by Climate Disruption." Rocky Mountain Climate Organization and Natural Resources Defense Council. July 2006.

Siegenthaler, Urs, et al. "Stable Carbon Cycle-Climate Relationship During the Late Pleistocene." *Science* 310 (2005): 1313–1317.

Stauth, David. "Global Warming Poses Risk to Pacific Northwest Snowpack, Ski Resorts." *Oregon State University News and Communications Services* 7 March 2006.

"Students recognized for outstanding energy projects." National Energy Education Development Project. 1 May 2007. http://www.need.org/needpdf/07pressindschool.pdf.

Tebaldi, Claudia, et al. "Going to the Extremes: An Intercomparison of Model-Simulated Historical and Future Changes in Extreme Events." *Climatic Change* 79.3/4 (2006): 185–211.

Texas A&M Student Counseling Services. "Top Jobs in Energy-Related Industries." www.scs.tamu.edu/articles/hotocs0805.asp.

Thomas, Chris D., et al. "Extinction Risk from Climate Change." *Natur*e 427.6970 (2004): 145–147.

U.S. Environmental Protection Agency. "Drinking Water." www.epa.gov/region7/kids/drnk_b.htm.

——. "Recycling." http://www.epa.gov/epaoswer/non-hw/muncpl/recycle.htm.

——. "Conservation." www.epa.gov.

——. Office of Mobile Sources: Fact Sheet OMS-18. "Your Car and Clean Air: What YOU Can Do to Reduce Pollution." August 1994. http://www.epa.gov/otaq/consumer/18-youdo.pdf.

"Waste-to-Energy Innovation." *WE Energies.* http://www.we-energies.com/environment/renewable_energy_biomass_tinedale.htm.

Westerling, A. L. "Warming and Earlier Spring Increase Western U.S. Forest Wildfire Activity." *Science* 313 (2006): 940–943.

Woodyard, Chris. "Honda Sees Possible Ethanol Breakthrough—New Microorganism Improves Efficiency." *USA Today* 15 September 2006.

Yeoman, Louise. "Venomous Snails Aid Medical Science." *BBC News Radio* 27 March 2006.

Ziska, L. H., et al. "Cities as harbingers of climate change: common ragweed, urbanization and public health." *Journal of Allergy Clinical Immunology* 111.2 (2003): 290–295.

Zwally, H. Jay, and Konrad Steffan. "Surface Melt-Induced Acceleration of Greenland Ice-Sheet Flow." *Science Express* 297 (2002): 218–212.

Web Sites

American Forest and Paper Association. www.afandpaorg.

Energy Star. www.energystar.gov/ia/partners/promotions/change_light/downloads/MayorToolkit.pdf.

Environmental Defense Fund. www.environmentaldefense.org.

Food and Agricultural Organization of the United Nations, FAOSTAT. www.faostat.fao.org.

Green dream jobs. www.sustainablebusiness.com/jobs.

Indianapolis 500. www.indy500.com/news/story.php?story_id=4105.

National Climatic Data Center (NCDC). www.ncdc.noaa.gov.

National Resources Defense Council (NRDC). www.nrdc.org.

The Nature Conservancy. www.nature.org.

Renewable Energy Access. www.renewableenergyaccess.com/rea/jobs/home.

Sierra Club. www.sierraclub.org.

U.S. Census Bureau, 2000. www.census.gov/population/www/socdemo/age.html.

U.S. Department of Energy. Energy Efficiency and Renewable Energy. www.fueleconomy.com.

——. Energy Efficiency and Renewable Energy, Alternative Fuels Data Center. www.eere.energy.gov.

——. Energy Information Agency. www.eia.doe.gov.

Renewable Energy Systems. www.res-ltd.com/wind-power/faqs.htm.

World Wildlife Fund. www.worldwildlife.org.

Interviews and Correspondence

Eric Chivian M.D., Director, Center for Health and the Global Environment, Harvard Medical School.

Dr. Heidi Cullen, The Weather Channel climate expert and host of *The Climate Code.*

Richard Fox, Surveys Manager, Butterfly Conservation Initiative.

Tim Greeff, Campaign Director, Natural Resources Defense Council Climate Center.

Dr. Susan Hassol, climate analyst and author.

Noah Horowitz, Senior Scientist, Natural Resources Defense Council.

Daniel A. Lashof, Ph.D., Science Director, Natural Resources Defense Council Climate Center.

Anne Lasker, parent and creator of Trashion Show.

Kenny Luna, eighth-grade teacher.

Dr. Gareth Marshall, climatologist, British Antarctic Survey.

Nigel Pervis, The Nature Conservancy.

Joel Reynolds, Director, Natural Resources Defense Council Marine Mammal Protection Program.

John Steelman, Campaign Director, Natural Resources Defense Council Climate Center.

Eric Wolff, British Antarctic Survey.

Photo Credits

Grateful acknowledgment is made for permission to reprint the following:

All illustrations, charts, and graphs by Stephen Schudlich.

Page iii, globe: NASA. *Page v, globe:* NASA. *Page vi, sky:* © Corbis Photography (RF)/Veer, CBP1001034. *Page viii, globe:* NASA; *compact fluorescent lightbulb:* © Albert Lozano/Shutterstock Inc., 1041557; *boy:* © Robert Recker/zefa/Corbis, 42-15289550. *Page ix, fall trees:* © AVTG/iStockphoto.com, 925210. *Pages xii–xiii, grass:* © jallfree/iStockphoto.com, 1933744.

Part 1

Pages 2–3, grass: © jallfree/iStockphoto.com, 1933744; *globe:* NASA; *blanketed chair:* © Johan Odmann/Johner Images/Getty Images, 72163467; *pizza:* © Vasko Miokovic/iStockphoto, 1933040. *Page 4, Whoopie Cushion:* © PunchStock, TOY04983-00; *cow:* © Joy Brown/Shutterstock Inc., 1881097. *Page 5, Popsicle:* © Kate Tero/iStockphoto 2004834. *Page 6, fossil:* © Dirk Wiersma/Photo Researchers Inc., SE8713. *Page 7, oil barrel:* © Michael Osterrieder/Shutterstock Inc., 2011086; *spark plug:* © ajt/Shutterstock Inc., 34807; *traffic:* © Steve Lovegrove/Shutterstock Inc., 555926. *Page 8, coal:* © Sally Wallis/Shutterstock Inc., 1758426; *flames:* © J. Helgason/Shutterstock Inc., 837032; *city lights:* © Carlos Sanchez Pereyra/Shutterstock Inc., 1026956; *pipeline:* © Reed Kaestner/ Corbis (RF/SCHL), CB023359; *match:* © William Mahnken/Shutterstock Inc., 500119; *snowy house:* © Carsten Madsen/iStockphoto.com 1402087. *Page 9, coal miner:* © Tyler Stableford/Stone/Getty Images, 200438538-001. *Page 10, smokestacks:* © Steve Cole/Photodisc Green (RF)/Getty Images, BU005598. *Page 11, steam engine:* © Michael DiMunno/Shutterstock Inc., 62546. *Pages 12–13, surfer:* © Joe Mcbride/Photographer's Choice/Getty Images, 200350671-002; *Page 15, tree:* © Martin Rueger/Image Bank/Getty Images, 200332564-001. *Page 16, Dome C overview:* Courtesy British Antarctic Survey. *Page 17, Dome C ice core:* Courtesy Chris Gilbert/British Antarctic Survey. *Page 19, iceberg:* © Frank Krahmer /Masterfile, 700-00557458; *The Wicked Witch:* THE WIZARD OF OZ © Turner Entertainment Co. A Warner Bros. Entertainment Company. All Rights Reserved. *Page 20, Polar ice cap:* NASA, Goddard Space Flight Center, Scientific Visualization Studio. *Page 21, permafrost:* W. K. Fletcher/Photo Researchers Inc., BC6337. *Page 22, clear-cut mountain:* © Art Twomey/Photo Researchers Inc., 6V4711. *Page 23, Will Ferrell:* Courtesy BWR Public Relations; *piggy bank:* © Boden/Ledingham/Masterfile, 700-00318694. *Pages 24–25, sea:* © Stockbyte (RF)/Getty Images, dv030411; *SpongeBob SquarePants* © 2006 Viacom International Inc. All rights reserved. Nickelodeon, SpongeBob SquarePants and all related titles, logos and characters are trademarks of Viacom International Inc. "SpongeBob SquarePants" created by Stephen Hillenburg. *Page 26, footprint:* © James Levin, DSC_3661. *Page 29 A, Reggie Bush:* © Sean Gardner/Reuters/Corbis, 42-17737181; *B, Jennifer Garner:* © Sheryl Nields/Icon International (photo provided by Management 360); *C, Shaun White:* © Bo Bridges/Corbis, 42-17259751; *D, Sheryl Crow:* Courtesy Chris Hudson; *E, Jim Lovell:* © Bettmann/Corbis, U1658271; *F, Leonardo DiCaprio:* © AP Photo/Kevork Djansezian, 04120207325; *G, Cedric the Entertainer:* © Don Tucci/Courtesy Entertainment Enterprises; *H, Laird Hamilton:* © Tony Friedkin/Sony Pictures Classics/ Zuma/Corbis, DWF15-575953.

Part 2

Page 32, muscle: © Tomasz Trojanowski/Shutterstock Inc., 2649385; *satellite view of Hurricane Katrina:* NOAA. *Page 33, Category 1 hurricane:* Courtesy PDPhoto.org, Waves 2002012014; *Category 3 hurricane:* Courtesy Jeff Williams/morgueFile.com, 85453; *Category 5 hurricane:* Courtesy Craig Toocheck/stock.xchng, 502911. *Page 34, cows:* FEMA News Photo/G. Mathieson, 314. *Page 35, typhoon:* © JTB Photo/Photolibrary, 141602129D. *Page 36, flooding:* © Royalty-Free/Corbis, CB031981. *Page 38, dry riverbed:* © Christopher J. Morris/Corbis, AAFR001149. *Page 39, dry, cracked earth:* © 2007 Gary Braasch/ILCP; *Map:* Jim McMahon/Scholastic. *Page 40, cornfield afflicted by drought:* © JP Laffont/Sygma/Corbis, 42-16984834. *Page 41, X-Games cyclist:* © Phil Ellsworth/ESPN. *Page 42, heat-exhausted dogs:* © BIOS Balcaen Claude/Peter Arnold Inc., 108415. *Page 43, spectators sprayed with water:* © Snaps/Action Press/Zuma/Newscom, zumaphotos 469368. *Page 44, abandoned beach house:* © 2007 Gary Braasch/ILCP. *Page 45, Tuvalu wave:* © 2007 Gary Braasch/ILCP. *Pages 46–47, Mt. Rainier:* ©

J. A. Kraulis/Masterfile, 700-00033972. *Pages 48–49, grass:* © jallfree/iStockphoto.com, 1933744; *poison ivy:* © Keith Spieldenner/Shutterstock Inc., 819211; *fall leaf:* © Tobias Machhaus/Shutterstock Inc., 2229998; *skier:* © Geir Olav Lyngfjell/Shutterstock Inc., 2821663; *ragweed:* © Steve Cole/Masterfile, 700-00193971; *hockey players:* © Photodisc (RF)/Getty Images, rbs1_54; *mosquito:* © 3D4Medical.com/Getty Images, 73337318; *bark beetle:* © Rod Planck/Photo Researchers Inc., 6Y6488; *pancakes:* © bluestocking/Shutterstock Inc., 2800454.

Part 3

Page 53, Map: Jim McMahon/Scholastic. *Page 54, walrus:* © Kevin Schafer/ILCP, 153181. *Page 55, emperor penguin:* © Kevin Schafer/ILCP, 121329; *dead polar bear:* © Doug Allan/Oxford Scientific/Photolibrary, OSF 20035979; *polar bears:* © Kevin Schafer/ILCP, 110459. *Page 56, polar bear:* © Wayne Bilenduke/The Image Bank/Getty Images, 200121503-001. *Page 58, blue whale:* © Francois Gohier/Photo Researchers Inc., BD8807. *Page 59, healthy coral:* © Darryl Leniuk/Masterfile, 700-00623405. *Page 60, bleached coral:* Courtesy Ray Berkelmans, Australian Institute of Marine Science. *Page 61, bleached coral:* Courtesy Ray Berkelmans, Australian Institute of Marine Science. *Page 62, Monteverde Cloud Forest:* © Kevin Schafer/Peter Arnold Inc. PA0071639; *golden toad:* Charles H. Smith/U.S. Fish and Wildlife Service, source #WO-2691-13. *Page 64, monarch butterfly:* © Royalty-Free/Masterfile, 616-00413874. *Page 65, Scotch Argus Butterfly:* © Laurie Campbell/NHPA, 00014702; *Ringlet butterfly:* © Sergey Chushkin/Shutterstock Inc., 1133407. *Page 66, Mt. Graham red squirrel:* © John Cancalosi/Peter Arnold Inc., PA1242871.

Part 4

Pages 70–71, U.S. Capitol Building: © Randy Wells/Stone/Getty Images, 454610-001. *Page 72, Portland bike lane:* © Jonathan Maus/BikePortland.org, DSC_1910. *Page 74, compact fluorescent lightbulb:* © Albert Lozano/Shutterstock Inc., 1041557; *girl:* © Steve Craft/Iconica/Getty Images, 200348188-002. *Page 76, wall with outlet:* © Creasence/Shutterstock Inc., 2915616; *Energy Star logo:* Courtesy Energy Star, U.S. Environmental Protection Agency. *Page 77, plugs with cords:* Anthony Berenyi/Shutterstock Inc., 2616366. *Page 78, paper bag:* © Photos.com, 8020375; *plastic bag:* © Stephen Stickler/Photographer's Choice/Getty Images, 200470838-001; *canvas bag:* © James Levin, DSC_4013. *Page 80, Muir Woods:* Walter Meayers Edwards/National Geographic/Getty Images, ngs0_8548. *Pages 82–83, sky:* © Corbis Photography (RF)/Veer, CBP1001034; *notepaper:* © Siede Preis/Photodisc (RF)/Getty Images, AA003104. *Page 84, sky:* © Corbis Photography (RF)/Veer, CBP1001034; *notepaper:* © Siede Preis/Photodisc (RF)/Getty Images, AA003104; *classroom:* © Stockbyte Photography (RF)/Veer, SBP0353011. *Page 85, school with solar panels:* Courtesy Glen Kizer for Foundation for Environmental Education. *Page 86, NYC city bus:* Courtesy Ernie Mauro, BAE Systems; *Prius:* Courtesy, © 2007 Toyota Motor Sales, U.S.A., INC. *Page 87, wheat field:* © Harald Sund/Photographer's Choice/Getty Images, 200364465-001; *flex-fuel car:* Josiah Cuneo/Courtesy greasecar.com. *Page 88, Indy 500:* Courtesy Indy Racing League, indycar.com, photographer Chris Jones. *Page 89, wind turbine farm:* © Rafa Irusta/Shutterstock Inc., 1242320. *Page 90, Dell-Winston solar car:* Courtesy Dell-Winston School Solar Car Challenge. *Page 91, Old Faithful:* © Emanuele Taroni/ Photodisc (RF)/Getty Images, AA019665. *Page 92, Grand Coulee Dam:* © Philip Gendreau/Bettmann/Corbis, GNGN388. *Page 93, wood chips:* © Elena Elisseeva/ Shutterstock Inc., 3039011. *Pages 94–95, sky:* © Corbis Photography (RF)/Veer, CBP1001034. *Page 96, sky:* © Corbis Photography (RF)/Veer, CBP1001034; *Gro Harlem Brundtland:* © Ralph Orlowski/Getty Images, 52193186. *Page 97, Eagles logo:* Courtesy Philadelphia Eagles; *Paul Frank logo:* Courtesy Paul Frank; *Ugg logo:* Courtesy Ugg Austrailia; *MTV logo:* Courtesy thinkmtv. *Page 98, Coldplay:* © Kevin Westenberg/Courtesy 3 D Management. *Page 99, globe:* NASA.

Pages 100–101, grass: © jallfree/iStockphoto.com, 1933744. *Page 102, Stopglobalwarming.org logo:* Courtesy Laurie David and The Tide Center. *Page 112, sky:* © Corbis Photography (RF)/Veer, CBP1001034; *authors:* Stacie Isabella Turk, Ribbonhead. *Page 113, sky:* © Corbis Photography (RF)/Veer, CBP1001034. *Page 114, Stopglobalwarming.org logo:* Courtesy Laurie David and The Tide Center.

Index

About the Authors

Laurie David is a global warming activist and the producer of the Academy Award-winning film *An Inconvenient Truth* and the HBO documentary *Too Hot Not to Handle*. She executive-produced *Earth to America!,* a primetime comedy special about global warming, which earned her a Gracie Allen Award for Individual Achievement. A trustee of the Natural Resources Defense Council, Laurie founded the Stop Global Warming Virtual March with Senator John McCain and Robert F. Kennedy, Jr. She was the first-ever guest editor of the green May 2006 and 2007 issues of *Elle* magazine. In 2006 Laurie published her first book, the bestseller *Stop Global Warming: The Solution Is You*. She also launched the Stop Global Warming College Tour with Sheryl Crow, on which they visited college campuses throughout the Southeast on a biodiesel tour bus.

Laurie David received the prestigious Stanley Kramer Award from the Producers Guild of America and a Humanitas Prize Special Award for *An Inconvenient Truth*. She has been honored with the Audubon Society's Rachel Carson Award, the Feminist Majority's Eleanor Roosevelt Award, the NRDC's 2006 Forces for Nature Award, and by Robert F. Kennedy Jr.'s Riverkeeper organization.

Laurie, a regular blogger on the Huffington Post, has been featured on such shows as *Oprah*, *Good Morning America*, and on CNN and has been profiled in numerous magazines, including *Vanity Fair*, which called her the "Bono of climate change." She lives in Los Angeles, California.

Cambria Gordon is an award-winning former advertising copywriter who now pursues children's writing full-time. Her credits include a nonfiction book, *Fifty Nifty Crafts to Make With Things Around the House*, and an episode for the award-winning animated Disney Channel series *Madeline*.

Cambria is an active environmentalist and lives with her husband and their three children in Los Angeles, California.